Marriage: A Loveseat for Two

ANDREW C. DAUBON

DEDICATION

This book is dedicated to the two "M's" in my life.

The first M is my grandmother Merilda, who laid a sturdy, robust and godly foundation in my life.

The second is my lovely wife Michaelia, who decided to marry me fifteen years ago when all I had was a roll up bed, an old Honda Civic, an entry level job and God. Your belief in me made it easy to believe in myself.

Thank you!

CONTENTS

ACKNOWLEDGMENTS

I want to thank my dad, Carl, step mom, Marlene, and the rest of my family for their prayerful support. I want to thank Mareen, Paulette, Beryl, Errol, Verna and the entire King's Chapel family who stood by my wife and I from the moment I proposed and long after we said our "I Do's."

I also wish to thank Bishop Randolph Scott who was the first to invest in my abilities as a leader, and my spiritual parents, Bishop Michael and Lady Ena Mitchell for their wise council, timely encouragement and their unrelenting love.

I must thank Bishop Errol Hall whose prophetic instructions paved the way for this book. A big "thank you" to the men and women of God whose unwavering care and concern have nurtured my confidence and challenged me not to settle.

I must give God thanks for the best church family one could hope for, the Celestial Praise Church of God, you have helped me live what I preach and have directly or indirectly helped to make this book a reality.

Finally, I want to thank my editor, Nicola Martin, whose linguistic finesse has masterfully fitted the many pieces of this project together for the good of the reader and to the glory of God.

THE BUZZ

"Bishop Andrew Daubon has written a remarkably engaging book that will tremendously benefit those who seek, or long for, a healthy and loving marriage. He skillfully weaves God's biblical framework for marriage with insightful, how-to guidelines that will strengthen and enrich the lives of couples who embrace these teachings. His real-life stories are relevant; his nuggets of wisdom are inspirational; and his "love seat for two" reference paints the perfect picture for what a loving relationship can be -- and should be. Through it all, he adroitly places this "love seat" on the foundational principles of *leaving, cleaving, oneness,* and *trust.* In fact, both single and married people should read and study this book to discover the joy and fulfillment a powerful marriage bond can offer."

Rev. Dr. W.C. Watson, Jr., DMin.
Senior Pastor, Canaan Baptist Church of Christ,
Springfield, MA.

"I appreciate Bishop Andrew Daubon's common sense approach to marriage and the way he helps Christians see that when God's principles are incorporated into our marriage, they can become beautiful, one flesh entities instead of until death do us part grin and bear it daily doses of bitter medicine. His chapter on biblical sex is especially enlightened."

Pamela Lagergren Williams PhD
Assistant Director of Developmental Education,
American International College
Adjunct Professor, Bay Path College

"'Marriage: A Love Seat for Two,' is a compilation of great insights by its author, Andrew Daubon, that gives the reader sound biblical foundations for a successful and fruitful marriage. It not only provides clear instruction for couples starting out on their journey into marriage, but also provides information to revitalize and redirect existing marriages."

Bishop Kenneth W. Trawick

Lead Pastor, Promise Land Ministries,

East Haven, CT.

"An easy-to-read, no holds-barred biblical perspective on the required approach for a successful marriage. By no means exhaustive, this book starts the conversation and provides several opportunities for self-evaluation."

Tricia-Gaye Cotterell

Juris Doctor Candidate, 2016

Nova Southeastern University

"Highly recommended for all ages, but especially for young couples in need of starting their marriage on a good foundation. Very detailed and yet to the point!"

Bishop Michael Mitchell

Senior Pastor, Kings Chapel Church of God

Hartford, CT.

"This book has the strong biblical foundation necessary for a successful marriage and is replete with humorous and practical illustrations. This is a must read for those seeking to portray God's ideal in marriage."

Bishop C. McLean
Founder & Pastor, Worship and Faith International
Fellowship (WAFIF)
Spanish Town, Jamaica.

"The subject of marriage is one of my favorite topics to teach on. Thus finding and reading wholesome material on marriage not only enriches my life, but adds to the collection of tools I have to use in my personal ministry to couples. "Marriage: A Love Seat for Two" is such a book. It is challenging, engaging, and thought provoking. It's not a book just to be read, but a book that couples should study together to bring both light and refreshing to their relationship."

Pastor Dean A. Brown
Christ Alive Christian Center
Bronx, NY.

FOREWORD

I find this book, "Marriage: A Love Seat for Two," compelling, as Bishop Andrew Daubon sets forth an agenda for any two people who really want to find significance in each other.

He knows that many of us were not prepared for this great leap but recognizes that a successful marriage is possible if we just make a little effort to understand the Heavenly Father's design and seek His support in this undertaking.

Marriages may be made in Heaven but they are worked on in the earth. Your marriage can be saved, supported and quickened if you take the advice offered in this book.

There is no need to reinvent the wheel when the unveiling of the revelation has been given by Andrew, who seeks to answer the question: Is there a foundation to undergird marriages that seem to be falling apart given the many challenges that are being presented in today's environment?

This book can save you so much trouble and irreparable frustration as you try to develop a healthy relationship. It will not only help those who are entering the union for the first time but it will be a support and foundation for those who want to restore the love and communion that may have vanished from the relationship.

Read it and you will fall in love again! I highly recommend it. It will have an impact.

Archbishop LeRoy Bailey, Jr.

Senior Pastor and Chief Executive Officer,

The First Cathedral

INTRODUCTION

For many people, Saturday night is often a time to relax and unwind after a tough week and an activity filled day. Saturday nights mean something else for me. It's typically the time I use to put the finishing touches on my sermon. During my preparation, I sometimes imagine the congregation's responses. I hear the "Amens"; I see the raised hands; I see the changing facial expressions as the people in the congregation make personal connections with different portions of the sermon. I visualize all of that before I ever preach the sermon. If I am honest, I have a deep desire to see my congregation respond to my sermon in a certain way.

Just as I desire a specific response from my congregation on Sunday mornings, God also has expectations of me on Sunday mornings. He wants me to be open to say what He wants me to say in just the way He intends it to be said. Simply put, my primary job as a pastor on a Sunday morning is to deliver the Word of God exactly as He gives it to me.

Creators are like that. If you have ever created anything to be used by others, you can relate to the deep desire to see that thing be used for its intended purpose. In fact, most creators go the extra mile to give us detailed manuals that instruct us on how to use their inventions. Whether that invention is a board game, an electronic appliance or a car, the creators take time to instruct us on how to use their products. Even articles of clothing have care instructions, e.g., dry clean only, or, wash in cold water on gentle cycle with like colors, etc. These instructions are specific, but they are critical if we are to use the product appropriately and get the best results. This is important to creators, but it is also important for us as consumers. Having instructions allow us to get the most out of the products we enjoy.

Just as instructions guard against abuse of the product, they protect us from being abused by or abusing ourselves with the product. We all know somebody (yours truly included) who has tried to assemble a product without the manual only to end up with extra parts and a product that does not work. Sometimes we cause unintentional damage to the product because we fail to read and follow the instructional manual.

Marriage can be seen as an invention or creation. I believe that God is its **Creator** and that mankind is the **consumer**. Like all inventions, marriage was created by its Creator to satisfy the needs of the consumer. In order to know the purpose and the "how to" of marriage, one should consult the Creator. Who better to consult about marriage than the one who created both the consumer (mankind) and the thing to be consumed (marriage)? As our creator, God knows us intimately. He knows what we need and how to meet our needs. This makes Him the uncontested and ultimate authority on the subject. Luckily for us, the Creator has made His instructional manual, known to us as the Bible, available to us.

Genesis 2:18 identifies the need for which marriage was made to satisfy. It states, "Now the Lord God said, It is not good (sufficient, satisfactory) that the man should be **alone**; I will **make** him a **helper** (suitable, adapted, complementary) for him." Gen. 2:18(AMP). The first need that the Creator identified was that the consumer, Adam, was alone. Adam had a beautiful garden and all kinds of exotic animals around him but he was still alone. He was missing companionship because nothing in his environment could relate to him at his level. To meet this need, the Creator decided to make or fashion, specifically for Adam, a companion.

Interestingly, the original word used for "helper," as it is used in

Genesis 2:18, denotes a person who joins someone else to assist in a time of hardship and distress. I find this explanation important to note because, in many cultures, the term "helper" is often used interchangeably with hired help or a maid. In the context of the above text, the term "helper" speaks more to companionship. Thus, the Creator fashioned woman as a specific companion for man, who, in this case, is Adam. Adam's response was one of happiness. "Adam said, this [creature] is now bone of my bones and flesh of my flesh; she shall be called Woman, because she was taken out of a man." Genesis 2:23(AMP). *It was love at first sight.*

I remember, after being married for four years, agreeing with the idea of my wife going to our native island of Jamaica to spend three weeks during the Christmas season without me. I must confess that that was the loneliest, longest and most distressing three weeks of my life. She had become such an integral part of my life that I had difficulty living without her.

I would guess that almost every wife reading this book has had numerous occasions when she has gotten a call or a text from her frantic husband at home trying to find something or asking how some basic kitchen appliance works. And, being equipped with telescopic lenses and a photographic memory, she is able to give her husband turn by turn directions to his missing cuff links or directions on how to use the rice cooker from 1500 miles away. I learned my lesson and fully agree with the Creator of marriage that it is not good for man to be alone. God's answer to any man being alone was and will always be the joining of that man with a special woman in marriage.

However, as with any other invention, if we are to get the most out of our marriages, we must get to know what the Creator says about marriage. We must get to know the instructional manual. This book is designed to help you get the most out of your marriage. After studying God's manual, I have uncovered four key components to a healthy marriage. These four components are what I refer to throughout this book as legs because they are foundational to any successful marriage. Marriage, I believe, is a loveseat for two: one man and one woman. The four components I refer to throughout the book are the legs that keep the loveseat from crashing to the ground. It is my prayer that you and your spouse will use this book to strengthen your marriage and that your loveseat will become more comfortable and secure.

I find a loveseat an appropriate metaphor for marriage because it is designed to seat two people who enjoy being in each other's company. It affords them the options of cuddling, sitting in the other's lap, lying on the other's shoulder, sitting face to face, sitting side by side and a number of other creative configurations. Each position on that loveseat could represent a different mood or stage of the relationship but what is important is that they are in it together. Marriage only works if both parties are in it together. To go back to our original analogy of the invention, the Creator, and the consumer, we can now say that marriage is a loveseat created by God for one man and his lady (the consumers). The focus of this book will be on the four legs on which this coveted loveseat rests, as ultimately, they are very important in making and maintaining a strong, cozy and durable loveseat (marriage).

1

THE FOUR LEGS OF THE LOVESEAT

God's intention for marriage is clear from the moment of its creation. That is why the foundational Scripture for this book is taken from that moment (the very beginning of the first marriage) in Genesis 2:24-25. This is where God gives us the key ingredients to making marriage work. It is from this Scripture that I arrived at the concept of the loveseat.

Having established that marriage is a loveseat exclusively for one man and one woman, the book goes on to lay out what I refer to as the four legs needed to support the loveseat. In Genesis 2:24-25 God said: "Therefore shall a man [1] **leave** his father and his mother, and [2] shall **cleave** unto his wife: and [3] they shall be **one** flesh. [4] And they were both naked, the man and his wife, and were **not ashamed.**" (KJV).

I must add here that Jesus also considered the above text fundamental in dealing with matters pertinent to marriage. In St. Matthew 19:4-5 when questioned about divorce, Jesus quoted the above instructions, which He ascribed to the Creator. To do justice to the above instructions provided by the Creator of marriage, I find it necessary to dedicate one chapter to each leg.

Before we dive into the other chapters, it is important that I point out something else that I have observed about the instruction. In the Scripture, the word "shall" precedes the first three instructions. The message that the Creator is conveying here is that to achieve the desired loveseat, there are three things that must happen: We must leave; we must cleave and we must be one flesh. When these three things are in place, they will naturally give birth to the fourth of not being ashamed.

A natural question that arises after such a forceful statement is: "Can my marriage survive without having all four?" The answer is "Yes." Your loveseat might be shaky and somewhat uncomfortable without any of the four, but, with the right adjustments, you will be able to improve the loveseat experience. Some marriages may have all four legs in place but still have some unsteadiness in the relationship. It could be that one or more of the legs may need some slight adjustments.

It is my hope that this book will show you how and where to make those adjustments to your loveseat, so that you can enjoy your marriage the way the Creator intended.

NOTES

2

LET'S GET OUT OF HERE

The first instruction God gives about marriage in Genesis 2:24-25 concerns leaving. This is the first leg of the loveseat. God says, "Therefore shall a man leave his father and his mother." Genesis 2:24(KJV). Leaving brings with it all kinds of emotions. No moment highlights this and brings these emotions to the forefront more than a wedding.

I have been playing an official role in weddings for roughly twenty

27

years. I have done everything from emceeing wedding receptions to meeting with prospective couples for premarital counseling to serving as the officiating minister of weddings. Over the years, I have had all kinds of experiences; some good, some bad, some funny and some very emotional. I have found that even at a wedding where the bride and groom seem to be a perfect match, emotions fly high on every side. This is because the moment both say, "I do," major changes begin to occur. The bride's father may feel that he has now lost his place as the main provider and protector of his daughter. He now has to trust and believe that this other man, the groom, will do for his daughter all that he did and more. For her part, the bride must now shuffle the order of priority of the men in her life. She must also leave the home and people with a proven track record of provision and security, and trust someone new to do the same in a place that is unfamiliar to her.

On the other side of the emotional fence is the groom's family. His mother, even while doing the last dance with her son at the reception, must deal with the fact that another woman is now number one in his life. Her son is leaving to have his own house and start his own family and the mother and son dynamic will never be the same. The groom, for his part, has to look at what he has to walk away from and what he is walking into. With just an "I do" and a signature, he has now signed up to be responsible for at least one other person for life. A man has entrusted him with his daughter and the world is watching to see how well he will handle this new responsibility. Many unanswered questions loom but this new husband and wife must leave their familiar places and venture into the unknown.

I know the above scenario is less and less typical here in the Western world as more and more people get married after they have already moved away from the parents' home (yours truly included), and modern day family dynamics are such that a bride may not have her father in her life to give her away. However, I have chosen this scenario because it is most consistent with the framework laid out by our Creator in the Instructional Manual. I must hasten to add also that the above scenario is often the most difficult transition as the newlyweds are both dealing with the anxiety of moving away from their parents for the first time and starting their new life together.

Leaving is also necessary for newlyweds where one or both parties lived on their own prior to marriage. In fact, leaving can be particularly challenging for the individual who has lived on his/her own prior to marriage, as the new relationship requires an abandoning of the single-life mentality. This person must leave behind the mindset that says, "I do what I want, when I want, how I want to, with no consideration to anybody else." In order to be in compliance with the Instructional Manual, both will have to leave "my way" behind, and latch onto "our way."

Not only is leaving a physical experience, but it also requires an emotional response. In this chapter, we will look at leaving from both a physical and an emotional perspective.

Moving Out: Leaving in the Physical Realm

Both the husband and wife must leave their respective families' worlds in order create one of their own. This leaving often means physical relocation, especially if living with family. Having a place to call your own is important in marriage because the parental home already has somebody who sets the tone for that home, usually the father or mother.

If a couple marries and remains in the home of either of their parents, they must submit to the authority in that home. This prevents the husband from assuming his role as leader of his house. A prolonged stay under parents' roof can have significant negative impact on the new groom's self image and confidence, as he never gets to truly exercise and develop his skills in setting the tone for his household. If living with the bride's parents, the bride may be torn and/or confused as to whom she owes her loyalty. She might also struggle to decide when to be a wife and when to be a daughter/daughter-in-law. There can be only one king and one queen in a home; therefore, in order for the newlyweds to become king and queen, they will have to establish their own domain/kingdom in a space of their own.

By definition, a king, is a man who has absolute authority over a kingdom/domain. To be successful, he must have people who are loyal to his rule. To be complete and for continuity, he must have a queen. Simply put, the husband's kingdom is his home. His kingdom is comprised of his family: those over whom he has authority and whose needs he is responsible for meeting. It is the physical leaving that makes it possible for the man to fully assume his role.

Putting the Pieces Together Once You Move Out

Leaving and establishing a kingdom is only the first step in the process. If the marriage is to thrive, both husband and wife must play a role in maintaining the kingdom. If the husband is king, the wife is his queen. If the wife is to play her role effectively, the husband must understand his role as king and even though the husband is king, the roles are interdependent. The effectiveness of the king's rule is directly impacted by how well his wife plays her role as his queen.

The reverse is also true. Sometimes it takes a wife to let the husband know that he is the king of their home, as not every husband comes into a marriage understanding his position and function. Take John, for example, who grew up without a father in the home. Growing up, John saw his mother doing everything in the home and had no way of discerning which roles would be a father's role. John, now a grown man, has never had the opportunity to observe a husband leading his family in a healthy way. After he marries the love of his life, he expects his wife to do all the things his mother did. As unbelievable as this may sound to some, John does not know that he is king and he does not know how to be king of his house. ***Ladies, if he doesn't know that he is your king, then don't expect him to treat you like his queen.***

This is one instance where proper premarital counseling is invaluable. This is also an occasion when a good wife can help. As queen, the wife becomes the primary manager of the home. She makes it a place of peace and contentment, a place he looks forward to coming home to. Please note that the house does not have to be large and extravagant for the husband to feel like a king; it's the atmosphere that his wife creates that generates that effect. He needs to get the sense that things are fairly organized, not chaotic. A wife can create an environment that makes it easy for her husband to step up and lead.

As with the husband, if the wife does not know that she is a queen, she is unlikely to treat her husband like a king. The home environment in which she grows up is critical in informing her perception of herself and her role. The queen needs to be lavished with affection. Affection is demonstrated in the manner in which things are communicated and in how she is treated. 1 Peter 3:7 states: "Likewise, ye husbands, dwell with them according to knowledge, giving honour unto the wife, as unto the **weaker vessel.**" (KJV).

The term "weaker vessel" is in no way a derogatory or sexist statement, but is rather emphasizing that the wife should be handled with special care. Comparably speaking, men could be likened unto the day to day dishes used in the home, while the wife is likened unto a fine China reserved for special occasions; both are vessels, but the fine China demands greater care in how it is handled not just because of its fragility but more so because of its value. Her king must discover her "love language" and use it often to communicate with her (Chapman, Gary). As you can see, it is critical that husband and wife recognize their roles upon entering marriage. Physical leaving allows both parties to fully occupy their respective roles, but it also exposes where there are insecurities or areas to be worked on in the relationship. That brings me to my next point.

Moving On: Leaving in the Emotional Realm

Leaving also has an emotional component. Many times, this can be more difficult to achieve than physical separation. The emotional leaving allows the couple to reprioritize the relationships in their lives, making the marriage their first priority. Failure to emotionally separate and reprioritize relationships will result in dysfunction. One spouse, for example, may be unable to make decisions within the marriage without his/her parents' input, leaving the other spouse to wonder who is running their marriage. If it is a case in which the wife is always consulting her parents, her husband may begin to feel like his wife does not have any confidence in his ability to lead their household. He may then ask himself the question: "If all the decisions are made by other people, what purpose do I serve?" **Very few people will stay in a relationship or marriage where they feel they are not needed**. That being said, please note that I am in no way suggesting that it is bad to ask for advice from parents and/or significant others. However, both parties (husband and wife) must agree on this course of action and the couple must be careful never to empower parents and/or significant others to make decisions in their marriage.

Failure to emotionally reprioritize can also bring about trust issues in the marriage. Consider Marcus, for example, whose family makes him feel obligated to cosign on a student loan for his younger brother, Matthew. Marcus goes ahead and cosigns without the knowledge or consent of his wife Becky. Becky only learns about it after Matthew drops out of college, defaults on the loan, and it shows up on Marcus' credit report. Becky is very disappointed by this unpleasant surprise and has trouble understanding why Marcus would make such a decision behind her back. Aside from that, she and Marcus must now determine whether they will allow their good credit to go bad or saddle themselves for several years paying back a debt that was not their own. Marcus' failure to emotionally reprioritize resulted in his making a decision that brought extra financial strain on the marriage and now causes Becky to be concerned about his loyalty and judgment.

Unlike physical leaving, the emotional reprioritizing is not an event that we can hire a moving company to do for us within a set timeframe; it's a process that can take months or even years. You cannot simply put emotions in boxes, load them onto a truck and have them delivered at your new emotional home. Emotional reprioritization is like learning a new way of doing something you are used to doing in a different way. It requires deliberate, consistent and repeated practice and reminders. Learning something new always comes with some degree of frustration, which will tempt us to revert to the old and familiar way. In the early years of the marriage, the couple must decide what parts of their individual past to keep and which parts to leave behind as they seek to fit together the pieces of their own unique loveseat. It really is like putting together a jigsaw puzzle, only more difficult because some of the pieces have to be adjusted in order for them to fit.

I have some friends, Clifton and Sharon, who almost abandoned their marriage because they couldn't get the pieces to fit. Clifton came from a home where his father's job was to provide food and shelter, fix whatever was broken and cut the lawn. His mother's job was to take care of the children, wash, cook and clean. Clifton never ever saw his dad doing laundry and never saw him with a broom. Sharon came from a home where both parents worked regular jobs, and both shared chores around the house. In fact, Sharon's dad always washed and ironed his own clothes. When these two lovebirds got married, both expected that their marriage would be a duplicate of their parents.' Clifton had no problem with Sharon working a regular job but got upset with her because she had stopped taking care of some of the chores within their small apartment. Sharon continued to do most of the housework, but stopped washing Clifton's clothes, thinking that Clifton was messy for allowing all of his dirty clothes to pile up. Clifton, on the other hand, thought that he married an untidy woman because she had stopped washing his clothes. The frustration between these two built to the point that they started thinking about divorce after only three years of marriage. Once they sat down together to express their individual frustrations caused by their unmet expectations, they both recognized that if their loveseat was ever going to work, they would each have to adjust the pieces they each brought to the marriage. Since neither of them could go back to their parents' house, they made the decision to emotionally separate from their parents' way of doing things. Once they left their parents' homes physically and emotionally, their only option was to figure out how to make the pieces of their loveseat fit together.

I hope it is becoming very clear to you why "leaving" (physically and emotionally) is a necessary leg of the loveseat called marriage. Leaving allows the couple the room they need to put the pieces of the loveseat together. It allows them to set the foundation of their unique relationship without outside interference. It allows them to custom-build their loveseat to meet their needs as a couple.

Earlier, we talked about how physical leaving allows each partner to occupy his/her role in marriage, but I also pointed out that leaving also exposes us to who we really are and shows us what we need to work on. These first years can be challenging in a marriage and can often result in a power struggle. Once a couple makes the decision to physically and emotionally leave their parents, they must quickly decide on and settle within their roles in order to avoid a power struggle.

We've Left. Now What?

Remember my friends Clifton and Sharon who had difficulty putting the pieces of their loveseat together? Well, once they both got an understanding of how different their childhood home experiences were, they had to work together to determine how their matrimonial home would operate; they had to settle the issue of "power" in the marriage. Power is simply the ability to get things done. In the context of marriage, power refers to the authority and ultimate responsibility held by the husband and/or his wife to make decisions within the marriage. In a marriage, power determines what is done, when it is done, and by whom it is done. The person with the power has the final word on the matter at hand. Couples sometimes enter marriage with different ideas about who should have power in their relationship.

Environment, social norms, culture, race, religion and education all bear influence on each spouse's philosophy on the matter of their and their spouse's role in the use of power in their marriage. Clifton and Sharon came into the marriage with differing views. Their failure to recognize this early and their inability to strike a compromise resulted in an impasse. Sharon refused to wash Clifton's clothes because she did not want to be his maid. She was protecting herself from Clifton's attempt to abuse his power as the husband. As a pastor and one who helps people troubleshoot their marriage, I know the issue of power in a marriage is extremely sensitive. Rather than reinventing the wheel, I turn to the reliability of to the Instructional Manual for guidance. Ephesians 5:22 states: "Wives, submit yourselves unto your own husbands, as unto the Lord." Ephesians 5:22(KJV). This text has been improperly interpreted and misused by many husbands over the years as a means to justify abusing their wives. I am reminded here, of an experience that one of my seminary professors had when he was the guest speaker at a weeklong conference where a number of pastors and their wives were in attendance. One morning, he got a frantic call from a pastor's wife who attended the conference. She needed the preacher to come over immediately. When the preacher arrived, the wife greeted him at the door with visible marks on her hands and legs. She had been beaten by her husband. She said he does this every couple of weeks with no provocation whatsoever. The preacher was both angry and surprised as he could not imagine why a husband would be so cruel to his wife.

The wife then said something that was even more troubling. She said that her husband's brother, who is also a pastor, does the same thing to his wife. These men were sons of a pastor. The preacher immediately summoned both husbands to a meeting to get to the root of the abuse. The brothers' response was shocking; they said their dad taught them that they should beat their wives on occasion just to make sure she remains in submission. Needless to say, their father beat their mother all through their childhood and they thought they were being faithful to what they considered to be "godly council."

Women who have experienced or witnessed ill treatment because of improper interpretation and subsequent abuse of the above text, may respond negatively to my bringing it up in this book. But before you stop reading or skip this portion of the book, please allow me a moment to explain its proper interpretation and give my opinion on the matter. The term "submit" or "submission" used in the text actually means to arrange in order of rank like in the military. In the military, a junior officer does not submit to his superior officer because the superior officer is a superior human being but because of his superior rank within the unit. Similarly, in the unit of marriage, the wife is asked to submit because God, the Creator of marriage, determined the order in which the unit must function if it is to thrive.

I often use the following example to explain this concept of submission: Consider the President of the United States, the most powerful man in the world. If he has to fly in Air Force One from Washington to Boston, he must submit to the flight crew to ensure safe arrival. Even though the president submits, he does not cease being himself; he still retains his ability to make powerful decisions even while aboard Air Force One. Similarly, **when the wife submits, she must not be stripped of her right to think and contribute, but each spouse must play his or her assigned role to ensure success of the whole.**

While the previously mentioned verse clearly places power in the hand of the husband, power does not function in isolation of but in conjunction with responsibility and accountability. The husband is placed as the head over his wife in the same manner that Christ is the head of the Church. Paul further states the kind of attitude the husband must assume in executing his role as the head. Ephesians 5:25 exhorts, "Husbands, love your wives, even as Christ also loved the church, and gave himself for it." Ephesians 5:22(KJV). When I first began thinking about finding a wife, this particular verse made me question my readiness. When I considered how much Jesus loves the church despite the headache and heartbreak the church gives to Him, it was difficult for me to see myself loving anybody that way. And when I finally got over that, I had even more consternation as the Scripture clearly expects a husband to give up his life for his wife if needed, as Christ did for the Church. It was at that point that I recognized that beyond feelings and desire, love is a decision to be fully committed to that one special person. God placed the husband above his wife to lead in love.

Despite western society's attempt to sell the idea that the best marriages are those with two heads (husband and wife), God's word maintains the husband's position as the only head, as anything with more than one head is abnormal and breeds dysfunction. As the head, the husband has the power to hand over authority of certain aspects of their lives as a couple, to his wife. Rather than having squabbles over who is the head, the couple should invest their energy in learning how to maximize their collective strengths, talents and abilities to achieve the "mission" of their marriage. For example, if the wife comes to the marriage as a better money manager, it would be unwise for her husband to insist on managing money matters on the grounds that he is head of the house. His wife taking the lead in this regard is not a knock against his leadership but a decision that will ultimately make him look good as her king. It is true that the husband is God's assigned head of the family, but in that role, the husband must know where, when and how to wisely allow his wife power to lead. Proper management of power within the marriage through good communication will make the marriage flourish.

You may have noticed in the biblical texts quoted on submission and love, that the wife's submission is not predicated on her receiving love from her husband; nor is the charge for the husband to love his wife contingent on his wife submitting to him. God intended for each spouse to simply do his/her part, not go through life responding to what his/her spouse does or doesn't do. God's intention is that both parties show their individual commitment to the "mission" of marriage. One of the telltale signs that a marriage is in trouble is when a husband or wife's actions are purely a reaction to their spouse's. You will hear the husband complaining that he does not show his wife any love because she does not respect him and the wife responds by asking, "How can I submit to a man who does not love me?" At this stage, the marriage has become nothing more than a game of tug-of-war. You can well imagine how sad it makes me feel to see good people in these situations because they have abandoned their God assigned responsibility.

Power Mismanaged

One very popular question that comes up when dealing with the issue of submission is: "Is there ever a situation where it is OK for a wife not to submit?" Let's see what answer the Instructional Manual provides. Paul, in his letter to the Corinthians states, "...the head of every man is Christ; and the head of the woman is the man." 1 Corinthians 11:3(KJV). Paul is stating here that the man's leadership of his wife is predicated on his following the leadership of Christ. Now this does not mean a wife should not submit to a non Christian husband; it means that she is expected to submit so long as he is not directing her into activities and decisions that violate God's instructions. Clearly stated, if a husband is leading his wife into things that are illegal or immoral, that wife has the right not to submit to his leadership.

The following true story presents another situation in which it is ok for a wife not to submit to her husband. There once was a very rich but brutish man named Nabal living in Palestine. Nabal made his riches by rearing large herds of goats and sheep. His wife was a beautiful and wise woman named Abigail. In those days, the livestock business was quite risky as thieves would sometimes attack, steal and even kill large numbers of the sheep and goats while they were in the fields grazing. Luckily for Nabal, his livestock grazed close to a military outfit led by a general named David. The proximity of David and his men insured the livestock against all attack, thus allowing them to multiply and make Nabal richer and richer. At least once per year, owners who were doing well would put on a celebration feast in honor of their employees. Nabal decided to do this, and during the celebration, General David sent messengers to Nabal congratulating him on his success but to also inform him that the military outfit was a major reason for his success. General David then made a modest request from Nabal to send him back something from the feast as a gesture of appreciation. Nabal, in a fit of rage, thought that David was trying to extort from him and sent back the messengers empty, hurling insults at their general. When General David got the news, he set out to raid Nabal's house, kill all the males in it, and take off with the spoils. In the meantime, word got to Abigail about her husband's cruel and foolish behavior and she decided to load a few donkeys with some food supplies and secretly went with servants to find

General David. She found him and his militia on their way to wipe out Nabal's household. When she saw him, she jumped off her donkey, bowed at his feet, apologized for the folly of her husband, and pleaded with him to accept her gift and change his mind about killing Nabal. General David was so moved by her gesture of kindness and her impassioned plea, that he changed his mind about going after Nabal. The next day, Abigail told Nabal what she had done to save everyone's life. The news was so dreadful to Nabal that he had a heart attack and died ten days later. Not long after, General David proposed to Abigail and she became his wife. This true story is found in 1 Samuel 25. Additionally, Nabal's name, translated, literally means "fool." Nabal was a fool because he made decisions that endangered the health and safety of his family. His reckless behavior and foolish actions put the lives of those he was responsible for in jeopardy. Abigail's decision not to submit to her husband in this case averted danger from her family. A wife is not obligated to submit to a husband who deliberately exposes his family in any such fashion. Such actions make that husband a fool. As paradoxical as it sounds, sometimes beautiful and brilliant women marry fools.

In Abigail's case, her marriage was arranged by her father and was unavoidable. In the western world, however, marriage is generally a personal decision. So how is it possible for today's Abigail to marry Nabal? Well, sometimes Abigail does not see the signs, and there are times when she simply ignores them, thinking that she can change Nabal. On other occasions, a man can become Nabal when he refuses to grow personally and intellectually. Take Jem and Alex, for example, who got married straight out of high school. They bought a house together and Jem nursed Alex back to health from an awful bout of cancer. As they both approached fifty years old, Jem gradually put on some extra pounds, partially due to medical issues. Alex began to hang with some younger guys who were not married; nor were they interested in any steady relationships. He began to desire the kind of girls that the other guys chased for entertainment. He then started to complain about Jem's weight. He even used it to belittle her. The taunting continued until Alex decided that he wanted a divorce. Jem surmised that if Alex was willing to trade in a stable and secure future with her for a fling, then he was no longer capable of being the head of her life. Thus, she granted him the divorce. Ten years later, Alex is approaching sixty years old without a home for himself and is by himself. Jem, in the meantime, has moved on; she is secure in her own home, surrounded by people who care for her and is in no rush to get into another relationship.

I took time out to talk about power in this chapter because once a couple makes the decision to leave, one of the first issues they must settle is that of power in the relationship. It is important that a man lead his wife in love and that his wife submits to his godly and prudent leadership. If the couple does not leave the parental home physically and emotionally, they will never settle the issue of power in their relationship and will be unable to truly fulfill their roles the way God designed them to. Instead, they will be under someone else's authority, which is sure to bring about marital dysfunction. Leaving is the first step to ensuring a proper balance of power in the marital relationship and is the first leg that the loveseat of marriage rests upon.

NOTES

NOTES

3

LET'S COME TOGETHER

O nce a couple has made the decision to leave the parental home, if their marriage is to survive and their loveseat is to be stable, they must work on securing the second leg of the loveseat by getting together in one accord or cleaving. In Genesis 2:24, not only does God say that a man must leave his father and mother, He also says that man *"shall **cleave** unto his wife."* Genesis 2:24(KJV) The word *"cleave"* means to cling to, stay close, to adhere, to be glued to. It creates a picture of two people glued together both mentally and physically. We will deal with the physical "oneness" that must occur in marriage in another chapter. In this chapter, we will talk about mental oneness or cleaving. Cleaving is a mutual decision to stick together irrespective of what life throws your way.

Cleaving produces a synergy or power of agreement. In Genesis 11 the people came up with the idea of building a skyscraper that would literally touch heaven. Their efforts were so serious that it warranted a visit by God Himself. After observing the people in action, God came to the following conclusion about the power of agreement: "Behold, they are one people, and they have all one language, and this is only the beginning of what they will do. And nothing that they propose to do will now be impossible for them." Genesis 11:6(ESV). Now if the Sovereign God says nothing is impossible (good or bad) when people have the power of agreement, then that's something we should all pay attention to. Jesus also shows how powerful it is when two people agree or cleave together around a particular thing. He says in Matthew 18: 19, "Again I say to you, that if two believers on earth agree [that is, are of one mind, in harmony] about anything that they ask [within the will of God], it will be done for them by My Father in heaven." (AMP). I find these two texts rather encouraging for those determined to have a successful marriage, as both speak of the undeniable power of agreement. The latter also indicates that when a couple is in agreement and are believers, God himself will give them what they ask for, so long as it is in His will.

Going back to the story in Genesis 11, we see where God found a way to defeat the power of agreement. He said: "Come, let us go down and there confuse their language, so that they may not understand one another's speech." Genesis 11:7(ESV). God disrupted the people's ability to communicate with each other and this yielded instant results. By the next verse, the people were scattered and the building project was abandoned. I have therefore concluded that communication is central if cleaving/agreeing is to occur. I will dedicate the rest of this chapter to looking at communication in marriage, as it is critical if a couple is to cleave together and secure the second leg in the loveseat.

Communication: Can You Hear Me Now?

I often tell the joke about little Johnny who went with his mom to a dinner, and while mom was in the middle of an interesting conversation with some of the guests, Johnny ran up to his mother, grabbing the front of his pants and shouting, "Mom I want to pee!" Mom, being a little embarrassed, took the toddler to the restroom, but told him that the next time he wants to pee, he should say, "I want to whisper!" A few months passed and late one night, little Johnny got up to use the bathroom but was afraid to go by himself. He went to his parents' room and tried to wake his mom to take him. He went to her side of the bed and shook her, saying, "Mom I want to whisper!" His mom, being very tired and half asleep, said, "Not now Johnny! Go whisper in your father's ear." Unfortunately for dad, Johnny obeyed his mother. Though this story is meant to be funny, it also illustrates that poor communication can be counterproductive, and can cause unintended injury to others whether physically or emotionally. Therefore, couples should always try to establish good communication in their marriage.

Good communication is a necessary ingredient in any relationship, especially that of marriage. A long time ago, my communications professor at Teachers' College said the following: "You have not truly communicated until the target audience receives the exact message you wish to convey." This means, that the communicator must learn to convey his/her message in a way that the audience will clearly understand. I can tell you that one of the quickest ways to get frustrated is to try to communicate to someone in a language they do not understand. Sadly, this happens in marriages more often than we think, even with couples that have been married for many years. Thanks to Gary Chapman's book, *The Five Love Languages*, we now know the five love languages, namely: quality time, acts of service, words of affirmation, gifts, and physical touch (Chapman). I have found that I am bilingual, in that I have a primary love language and a secondary one. My wife has one primary and two secondary love languages. I cannot tell you how this information has simplified and enriched our communication because we are able to meet each other's needs efficiently by using our preferred love languages to communicate with each other. Recently, I was counseling with a couple that just could not get on the same page with their communication. I had them do a love language assessment, and to our collective surprise, they both share the same love language. This discovery really helped to solve much of their frustration as we further discovered that they often wanted the same things but did not know how to best to communicate their desires.

Regardless of what a woman's love language is, she needs to be made to feel like a queen. A queen needs to be affirmed by her king and needs to be reassured that she is most beautiful, despite what outsiders may think. There are times in the marriage when the queen may need more frequent reminders of her beauty like during pregnancy or during bouts of illness. Her husband's job is to always make her feel secure and uncontested in her position. A sure way to do this is for her king to be perpetually consumed by her inner beauty, her mind and her body. It excites her to know that she is the only one he wants to "light his fire." She revels in the fact that she satisfies him. We will delve further into the sexual component of marriage in a later chapter.

Communication involves what is said and what is not said. It also involves how and when something is said. I have had instances in my marriage when I speak to my wife in what I believe to be a normal tone, only for her to ask, "Why are you shouting at me?" It took me a while to figure out that my wife was paying attention to more than the volume of my voice, but also the tone. My tone communicated more to her than the actual words that I was using. My tone said I was upset, and her asking why am I shouting, was her way of asking: "What are you upset about?" I have discovered that good communication is enhanced by the right timing, tone and attitude. It also involves expressions of love, respect, honesty, support, self-disclosure and sensitivity to the feelings of one's spouse. Good communication minimizes the need for and incidents of "mind reading." I often tell couples never to assume that your spouse knows what you want. Rather, it is your responsibility to make your desires known as clearly as possible. This applies to all aspects of the marriage.

In order for good communication to take place, the couple must be well aware of their differences. Women typically have conversations to connect, while men typically talk to troubleshoot problems. An easy way to get around this issue is for the wife to preface her conversation by saying: "Honey, I need to vent right now; I don't need any problem solved." Once the husband hears this, it relaxes him, and he is able to give her his full attention. We must train ourselves to be active listeners by listening to what is said and focusing also on what is being communicated through body language.

June Hunt, author and radio program host, in her expansive collection of counseling manuals called *"Biblical Counseling Keys,"* includes a section titled "Communication: The Heart of the Matter." In this section, she explains that communication in a marriage is ranked the highest level of communication. She believes that at this level there must be freedom from all fear of judgment or rejection, allowing for complete emotional connection with one's spouse. It requires complete openness and honesty, where deeply held beliefs and feelings are totally expressed. Two hearts are joined, two spirits are united and feelings are reciprocated. There is mutual understanding and empathy. Hunt concludes that this level of communication takes hard work because it is much more difficult to communicate heartfelt emotions than it is to communicate mere facts (Hunt). I agree wholeheartedly with Hunt on this and further believe that communication is likely to improve as a couple spends more and more quality time cleaving to each other. Remember the definition of cleaving given at the beginning of this chapter, to be glued to? Well, the strength of that kind of bonding can only improve the more the couple are physically with each other. The stronger the bond, the stronger the marriage will be.

Litzinger and Gordon have published a number of research pieces on the subjects of marriage, relationships and communication. In one such publication, in the *Journal of Sex & Marital Therapy,* they report on studies showing that communication is consistently and significantly related to couples' satisfaction. Those same studies also revealed that dissatisfied couples, seem to lack skills needed to communicate effectively. Such deficits tend to make one defensive or withdraw when faced with conflict or disagreements, which further impairs the couple's ability to solve problems and resolve conflicts

(Litzinger and Gordon). Shortly after I proposed to my wife, we became the focus of many people's attention. These people thought it was their responsibility to give us marital advice. I remember one couple inviting us to their home for dinner after church one Sunday to give us "advice." Right after dinner, the wife drew close to her husband and announced, with a huge expression of pride on her face, that throughout their many years of marriage, they had never once had a quarrel. I have to confess that after that statement, I did not hear anything else that this couple said. I knew immediately that this couple had nothing to offer me because their marriage was not based in reality. I concluded that somebody in that marriage was not being honest and was simply going along with whatever the other person desired. How else could two people who came from two different life experiences come together and never have conflict of ideas and opinions? This couple had very little conflict resolution skills because their marriage was all about conflict avoidance. Communication skills such as active listening, empathy and loving confrontation are like muscles; they get stronger the more they are used. It is important for couples, especially newlyweds, to know that conflict is not necessarily bad; it is an opportunity to grow.

One conflict resolution skill that is absolutely key in every successful marriage is that of amnesia. For this discussion, I define amnesia as the ability to forget past wrongs that were sufficiently dealt with and dismissed. Granted, the couple must recognize that when one person errs in the relationship and sincerely asks for forgiveness, the victim deserves to be able to resolve the matter in his/her own time and cannot be rushed to forgive. That being said, once the victim forgives, he/she has given up his/her right to keep dredging up the past every time there is a new conflict. The only time bringing up the past is warranted is if the guilty party keeps repeating the same offense. I have found that in many troubled marriages, the issue is not the offense that was committed, but the inability and sometimes refusal of the couple to move past the past. True repentance (i.e., sincerely turning away from), along with preventative action steps to ensure the action won't be repeated, warrants forgiveness. If we fail to forgive, then our marriage will be submerged in a cesspool of bitterness and will ultimately die.

When a marriage is going bad, the communication is usually the first thing that suffers. Every conversation becomes a battle with the ultimate goal of proving the other spouse wrong. While one spouse is talking, the other is busy planning his or her response and pays little attention to what is being said by the other party. It is particularly heartrending to see Christian marriages going bad because couples use the "truth" to tear down rather than to build up. They each forget that when they hurt their spouse, they hurt themselves. This is because, in marriage, the two are one flesh. Take Sally and John who have been married for 27 years. John is having potency issues due to side effects from high blood pressure medication he takes, and Sally has had weight gain due to medication she is taking for depression. Sally chooses to tell John the "truth" in anger and frustration, that he does not satisfy her sexually anymore, but John hears more than the truth; he hears that he is no longer a real man. John, feeling like his manhood is under attack, responds with some "truth" and blames his lack of performance on the extra pounds Sally has put on. He accuses her of being sexually repugnant. Good communicators would convey all of the above in a loving way and with the intention of working towards a solution. Poor communicators, on the other hand, end up playing the blame game. Poor communication breeds marital dysfunction and causes the loveseat to wobble and become unstable and uncomfortable. If the marriage is to thrive, we must ensure that the second leg of the loveseat, cleaving, is fully operational through effective communication.

NOTES

NOTES

4

LET'S GET IT ON

In the previous chapter, I said that cleaving is a mental process and that this coming together in agreement is a necessary component of a healthy marriage. That is the second leg of the loveseat. Once a couple commits to each other by leaving and figures out how to make it work by cleaving, it makes it possible for the third leg of the loveseat to be built. This is the physical component of coming together in marriage, and it is critical if a couple is to achieve the oneness the Creator intended them to have. In our foundational Scripture, after God talks about leaving and cleaving, He says, *"and they shall be **one** flesh."* Genesis 2:24(KJV). Oneness takes time to develop. When I think of oneness, I always remember a couple I knew in my home of Jamaica. For the purposes of this conversation we will call them Mr. and Mrs. Dawson. Like so many couples I know, Mr. and Mrs. Dawson were opposites. Mr. Dawson was quite rough and often blunt with people, but his wife was a gem. Although she was a no-nonsense person, her magnetic personality always pulled in both old and young alike. I still remember how, as a young man, I would observe these two together and see how Mr. Dawson always seemed to mellow out when Mrs. Dawson was around. There was just something about this couple that always intrigued me. How is it that so many people feared or even disliked Mr. Dawson, yet his wife loved him endlessly? There was no doubt that these two were made for each other. They even started to look alike. Many years later, Mrs. Dawson got ill and passed away. Not long after, Mr. Dawson, though in good health, suddenly passed away. Mr. Dawson simply did not know how to live without his wife and had no desire to learn to do so. This couple developed a synergy or **oneness** that made them unable to live without each other.

Soul Ties

Marriage is consummated by sexual intercourse, which is the ultimate physical display of the two becoming one. During sexual intercourse, a powerful connection, also called a soul tie, is established. This connects a husband and wife and causes the two to be drawn together for mutual sexual pleasure and fulfillment. A soul tie is so powerful that it can cause the couple to be irresistibly sexually attracted to each other and enjoy blissful sexual experiences even amidst difficulties in the marriage. I am well aware that many couples who get married do not do so as virgins. Therefore, I must speak a little about how soul ties are formed and how entering into a marriage with soul ties with people other than your spouse can be an obstacle in the marriage.

Simply stated, a soul tie is the bonding together of two or more people in the area of their mind, emotions and will (their souls). Because this tie is invisible, it is best detected in the behavior of those involved. It is also worth noting that not all soul ties are sexual in nature; some are emotionally driven where people seem almost addicted to the company of others and often begin to behave like them. Proverbs 22:24-25 warns, "Make no friendship with an angry man; and with a furious man thou shalt not go: Lest thou learn his ways, and get a snare to thy soul." (KJV). The expression "snare to thy soul" refers to a soul tie. The principle laid out in the above text does not apply only to anger but to other personality traits or behaviors, both good and bad. A soul tie can therefore be good or bad. Since the focus of this chapter is on oneness within marriage, we will take a closer look at sexual soul ties.

Because the Creator designed sex to enhance oneness within a marriage, the soul tie established in the marriage is blessed by God. Sex outside of marriage is sin, and sin gives demonic spirits legal right to attach themselves to those engaged in premarital or extramarital sex. A soul tie is also established in those cases, but they occur without God's blessing. Paul reminds his audience of what the Instructional Manual says in 1 Corinthians 6:16: "Do you not know that the one who joins himself to a prostitute is one body *with her*?" For He says, "The two shall be one flesh." (AMP). There is no other human activity in which we are more exposed to a soul tie than through sex. Therefore, when a person engages in sex with multiple partners, a soul tie can be established with each partner, regardless of whether the relationship is casual or serious.

There is a line in the chorus of a 1985 hit song made popular by Paul Young that speaks to what a soul tie does. It says "Every time you go away, you take a piece of me with you." The reality here is that sex is never ever casual, and premarital and extramarital sex is never safe because sex establishes lifelong ties among the participants. What is even more frightening is that a person can become tied to people they do not know because of their sex partner's previously established soul ties. This occurs because the soul tie does not automatically die when the relationship in which it was established ends. As a result, many married couples find their marriage seemingly crowded by people who are not even physically there. Take Suzette and Alex for example. They both had previous relationships in which they were sexually active. Soul ties were established and were never broken. The couple has found that no matter how good Alex is to Suzette in bed, he always falls short of Suzette's expectation. He's tried every trick in the book, and nothing seems to work. What Alex doesn't know is that Suzette has never gotten over her first love, Dean, who took her virginity. And so, every time she has sex, she goes back to that first time with Dean in her mind and emotions, hoping to duplicate the experience. This never happens, hence the constant let down. Poor Alex does not know it, but until Suzette cuts her soul tie to Dean, he will continue to fight against an invisible foe that is impossible to defeat.

The fact that soul ties survive failed relationships is also the reason why a man and a woman can break off their relationship and communication for years yet cannot resist each other sexually the moment they see each other again. It is always baffling to sometimes see brilliant and beautiful women who are woefully tied to men that will never leave their wives. They try desperately to justify their commitment and loyalty to men who they know will never be committed and loyal to them. This is how a soul tie works.

Set Me Free

The question now becomes, how does one break negative soul ties? It will take what I call the three "R's" - recognize, repent (and forgive) and renounce. You must *recognize* the pattern of behavior that has developed since your encounter with the person(s) you were sexually active with. Then, you must *repent and forgive*. Having identified the wrong that you have done, you must repent to God of those acts and forgive the perpetrator(s) if you feel you were wronged in the process. I must add here that repentance is not just saying I'm sorry, but it is the turning away from sin (that for which you are sorry). You must be specific about what you are repenting from and what you are forgiving others of. Finally, you must **renounce** all of what you did and said to help establish the soul tie. To renounce is to relinquish and abandon all connections to toxic relationships or soul ties. Renunciation requires both action and verbalization. It will require that you get rid of gifts, pictures, and things that connect you to or take you back to the experience. Please note that children are an exception to this rule and should never be abandoned as a means of breaking a soul tie.

"Death and life are in the power and the tongue." Proverbs 18:21a (KJV). That which we declare can become our reality. Therefore, you will need to renounce ill-advised pronouncements as well. Statements like "Nobody can ever love me the way you do," or, "You will always have my heart," or, "I will never find anyone who can do me the way you do," help to seal a soul tie, and must be renounced to undo it. It helps to be specific when you do this, so you will have to call the names of the people you are cutting ties from. You must renounce all of this, and command the soul ties to be broken in the mighty name of Jesus. Because sexual demons are often involved, people sometimes need to fast and pray about this and may even need to seek the help of their Spirit -filled pastor to be fully delivered. If you are not a Christian, breaking soul ties is another good reason to receive Jesus as Lord and Savior of your life, for only then will you have full authority to use His name and get results.

I took the time to speak to the issue of soul ties because it is impossible for any couple to achieve oneness if one or both of them are tied to other people. Oneness is meant to be the reality of the couple both inside and outside of the bedroom. As with sex, oneness is best achieved when the couple is deliberate about spending time with each other, knowing each other and growing together. Oneness is a process, not an event. You can know that a couple is achieving oneness when they begin to lovingly finish each other's sentences, when they can carry on a nonverbal conversation while at opposite ends of a crowded room, and, sometimes, they even begin to resemble each other. *Oneness is a beautiful thing.* Having dealt with the issue of sex and soul ties outside of marriage, we will now look at sex within the confines of marriage, the way the Creator intended for it to be used.

The Church and Sex

Let us return to our foundational text where God said, "Therefore shall a man leave his father and his mother, and shall cleave unto his wife: and they shall be one flesh. And they were both naked, the man and his wife, and were not ashamed." Genesis 2:24-25(KJV). The phrase "they shall be one flesh" has spiritual implications, but it also speaks to becoming "one" sexually. Additionally, although God, in Genesis 1, commanded mankind to be fruitful and multiply, the intent of sex is more than a childbearing exercise. It is a unique medium through which a man and his wife bond. The text goes on to say that they were both naked and were not ashamed. God intended marriage to be a union where the couple is free to be themselves.

The church, for many years, has rendered sex a taboo, mostly because of how society has desecrated it and because of the sullied image that has been attached to it. Inadvertently, the church seems to have bought into the notion that sex is dirty. Consequently, many wives view sex as a duty to be performed and not as something to be enjoyed. One of the things that my wife and I tackle while doing premarital counseling with brides to be (especially those with little to no exposure to sex), is to help prepare them to make the mental transition where sex is concerned. Because they have spent all their lives (up to this point) doing everything to stay away from sex, they must now begin to understand that when they get married, it is ok and good to engage in sex with their spouses. We also find that those with previous negative sexual experiences need help in making the transition as well. After having joint discussions with the husband and wife to be, my wife and I usually conclude the premarital sessions with her taking the future bride out for a one on one trip. On this trip, my wife has a woman-to-woman conversation with the bride about inhibitions the bride may have around the act of sex itself.

Included in the trip is a visit to a specialty store to purchase items that will enhance the lovemaking experience, such as massage oils, candles, lingerie etc. I must report that so far, the feedback has been quite positive as to how helpful this exercise has been for brides on their honeymoon and beyond.

Thankfully, many of our churches have begun to make great strides in correcting our attitudes about sex and have embarked on re-educating the body of Christ. Today, the topic of sex is even spoken about from the pulpit and is discussed in detail in marriage enrichment seminars. However, from time to time, there are those situations where sex, or the lack thereof, is a major issue in a marriage. Sex, just like money, can be wrongly used as a means of reward or punishment, a tool of manipulation and control. Often, it's women who employ this tactic; many times due to "advice" they receive from older women who are supposed to be more experienced and wiser. I must add here that some men have also latched onto this practice of using sex as a tool to reward and punish.

Up until a few years ago, I was not aware that the withholding of sex was something that men do and had a challenge containing my incredulity the first time this came to light in a session with a couple. Perhaps it's my Jamaican upbringing, but I am still surprised every time I come across this issue of a husband withholding sex from his wife. Every case I have seen of husbands withholding sex has involved the husband's desire to exert control over his wife. I have observed, however, that the withholding of sex tends to affect men differently from women. Men generally tend to see it as punishment, while women tend to see it as something more serious. Men, therefore, will either resort to serving their sentence in the "dog house," or will try to do something to get their "crime" expunged. Rarely do men consider the denial of sex as a knock against who they are. Women, on the other hand, tend to believe that denial of sex is an indication that they are no longer sexually attractive or that they are not "performing" up to par. For women, it can quickly become a self-esteem crisis and can leave scars long after the denial has stopped. This abuse of sex, I believe, results from couples not knowing what our Instructional Manual says about the subject of sex. Paul speaks quite clearly of the sexual expectations within a marriage. This is how he makes his case in his letter to the Corinthians:

> It's good for a man to have a wife, and for a woman to have a husband. Sexual drives are strong, but marriage is strong enough to contain them and provide for a balanced and fulfilling sexual life in a world of sexual disorder. The marriage bed must be a place of mutuality—the husband seeking to satisfy his wife, the wife seeking to satisfy her husband. Marriage is not a place to "stand up for your rights." Marriage is a decision to serve the other, whether in bed or out. Abstaining from sex is permissible for a period of time if you both agree to it, and if it's for the purposes of prayer and fasting—but only for such times. Then come

back together again. Satan has an ingenious way of tempting us when we least expect it." 1 Corinthians 7:2-6(MSG).

Paul addresses a myth that has managed to survive many years in the church. It is the myth that sex is about satisfying the needs of the husband only. Though this text was written in the context of a male dominated world, Paul made it clear that both spouses have a right to be sexually satisfied. I often say, if the husband is the only one enjoying sex, then, chances are, he is doing something wrong. A husband's ultimate fulfillment should be to know that his wife experiences the euphoria of sex that he experiences because, as indicated in the text, satisfaction is a two way street.

In their work in *The Journal of Sex & Marital Therapy*, Litzinger and Gordon mention research showing that personal sexual satisfaction in marriage, knowing that one's spouse is being sexually satisfied and the frequency with which a couple engages in sex are positively associated with marital satisfaction. They also cite another study, which revealed that "sexual satisfaction and overall well being are inextricably linked" (Litzinger and Gordon). Sex has been shown to have many "non bedroom" benefits, including lowering stress, lowering the risk of heart attacks, burning calories, managing or eliminating pain and improving sleep. My wife and I were doing a marriage session recently at a church in New York, and I told the congregation that we got new wedding rings for our fifteenth anniversary. I jokingly mentioned how much of a Trinitarian I am, in that I deliberately picked out a ring for myself with three stones just to remind us to have sex at least three times per week: one for the Father, one for the Son and one for the Holy Ghost. Right then, the host pastor made an announcement: his wedding ring had all of ten stones. Every husband in that church looked at the pastor with ten times more respect. The bottom line here is that sex within the confines of marriage was made by God to be enjoyed as often as the couple desires.

The Bedroom: No Place for Boredom

As humans, whenever we engage in anything on a regular basis, we run the risk of it becoming boring. Boredom occurs when things are done the same way, at the same time, in the same place, all the time. A simple change in a couple of the above mentioned components can often solve the issue of boredom. As a couple, you have to be willing to try new things, such as: new provocative lingerie, scented lubricants, candles, music, and different sexual positions. Christian couples should know that they will not go to hell for trying positions other than the missionary position. Trying different positions may give staying power to husbands experiencing premature ejaculation and could help wives experience orgasms as well. Couples should not be shy about talking to their doctor about any and all sexual dysfunction and discomfort as the experience is meant to be enjoyed, not endured.

Communication in the bedroom is very important as well. Do not wait for your spouse to read your mind; say what you like and don't like, say what you want more of and less of. Sometimes you may need to guide your spouse's hand to where you need to be touched and demonstrate how you want to be touched. The subject of lovemaking should not be a touchy subject; talk it over with each other at the right time and with love. Also, since you pay mortgage/rent for the whole house, you are at liberty to experiment in different places in the house, including the shower, tub, staircase, back porch (if it's private enough) etc. Couples with children may not be as liberal, but they need to ensure that a master lock is on the master bedroom door. Lock the door when you need to retreat there to "master" some things. Another way to keep the spunk alive in the bedroom is to read books on lovemaking. I would caution, however, against pornographic movies and publications due to their addictive nature and due to spirits that lurk in and around that particular industry.

Not Now Honey, I'm Pregnant

Going back to what Paul stated in 1 Corinthians 7:2-6, we find that our Instructional Manual gives only one reason for abstaining from sex within a marriage; *and that reason is not pregnancy.* The only reason supported by Scripture is when either or both persons go on a fast. And even in this case, the decision is a mutual agreement with a predetermined time limit. Paul is careful to mention a timeframe to guard against the Devil bringing temptation from outside that can potentially destroy or significantly weaken the marriage. I chose to draw attention to the issue of pregnancy, because, once again, some wives are sometimes led to believe that not having sex for the duration of the pregnancy is a small price their husband has to pay for "knocking" them up. This, my friends, is a very dangerous assumption, as studies have shown that infidelity in a marriage is more frequent during a wife's pregnancy. Wives reading this may get quite upset as to the gross insensitivity and heartlessness of those husbands. While there is no justification for infidelity, we must take seriously the warning Paul gives in the above quoted text. As a practical matter, wives should recognize that it is quite dramatic for a husband to go from having sex three times per week to zero for 4-6 months during pregnancy, plus additional time after the baby is born. Let me say here that the husband must appreciate the many physical, emotional and hormonal changes his wife experiences during pregnancy. He should not expect her to necessarily have the energy or desire to maintain the sexual frequency he may have become accustomed to before she became pregnant. His wife, however, must also remember that his needs never go away during the pregnancy, and she must do her best to address those needs.

I'll take a Rain Check

It is said that "men give love to get sex and women give sex to get love." Sex, for most wives, is not just physical, but it's also about connecting emotionally. A wife, therefore, needs to know that her husband doesn't just want her body, but all of her. She must feel that their time together is not always about fulfilling her husband's biological needs. Sex, for her, must also be about his desire to be one with her in the most intimate of ways. There is no denying that what happens the other 23 hours of the day bears impact on what goes on in the bedroom. A husband that constantly communicates love to his wife throughout the day will find that his wife will make special accommodations for him, even when she is very tired, busy or not feeling well. While I am on the topic, husbands, if we chip in more around the house, we may find that our wife is less and less tired, and more available for sex. A wife should also know that if she is always seeking to please her husband, on the occasion when she is really not up to it, a loving husband will understand. Another thing that can be quite helpful on those rare occasions is a "rain check." Rain checks are a promise to deliver on something later that I am not able to do right now. Wives, if you have a track record of honoring those rain checks, with a little extra something to go with it, your husband will gladly take the rain check on most occasions. The rain check is a promise that later will be greater.

Baby Don't Stop

In chapter one, I introduced the concept that a man should be king in his own house. Well, every king desires his queen to be the envy of the kingdom. This means that she must always be attractive to him. I once met a girl who was engaged to be married. During that time, she was quite meticulous about what she ate and stayed in good shape for her husband to be. One day, while having a conversation with her about the wedding, she informed me that once she is finally married, she will no longer put so much effort in staying in shape or remaining attractive because her husband will be stuck with her regardless of how she looks. Needless to say, I ran into her some years later only to find that the marriage broke up because the husband cheated on her with someone else. While I certainly do not condone cheating for any reason whatsoever, the moral of the story here is that our behavior while courting really is a promise to the would be spouse of what to expect from us in marriage.

Men must also put the work in to remain in shape for themselves and for their wives. Husbands, we must pay attention to the aspects of our physique that our wives consider important. This includes how we look and even what we wear. Being attractive applies to what a woman wears to bed as well; she must have sex appeal. Sometimes the hottest sex appeal is getting into bed the way Adam was introduced to Eve; they were both naked. When Adam first saw Eve, he exclaimed: "She shall be called wo [ah]-man (emphasis added)." Genesis 2:23(KJV). I don't believe he was only happy that he finally had somebody to talk to. I believe Adam was awestruck by her physical beauty. This woman made him feel feelings he never knew he had and woke up body parts that he never knew could be aroused. Adam immediately had the "urge to merge." A man's instinct to be visually stimulated does not diminish even with age. Hence, wives must invest in garments that accentuate their assets and make them feel confident. A wife that exudes confidence is attractive.

Confidence is like an expensive perfume: desired when used in moderation, overbearing when used in excess, and unnoticed when not enough is used. A wife must not only look good; she must also feel good about herself, as looking good and feeling good are often correlated. Couples need to know that they owe it to each other to retain their attractiveness. The moment they begin to take each other's preferences for granted is the moment oneness in the marriage begins to weaken. Your loveseat will not be as comfortable if the oneness leg is impaired or missing.

NOTES

5

LET ME COVER YOU

O ur loveseat is nearly complete. We have talked about the leaving that is necessary to establish marriage, the cleaving that mentally unites a couple, and oneness, the sexual connection which bonds a couple physically. If our loveseat is to be balanced, however, we must have one final leg in place. This leg is crucial and makes the loveseat capable of bearing the emotional, spiritual and physical weight of the couple. This leg is trust: easily broken but difficult to repair. The latter part of our foundational text states: "And they were both naked, the man and his wife, and were **not ashamed.**" Genesis 2:25(KJV). Unlike the other three legs, this one is not preceded by the word "shall," which means it was not an order from God but an observation that He made after Adam and Eve had secured the first three legs of their loveseat. Trust, therefore, is the by-product of leaving, cleaving and oneness combined.

All three legs work together to establish trust, but the other three are unable to function without it. Understand that this level of trust is unlike all else. To this point, a married couple may have had people in their individual lives that they trusted to varying degrees. They trusted the counsel of parents; they trusted the instruction of a teacher; they trusted the leadership of a boss; they trusted the integrity of their pastor, but none of those relationships demand the comprehensive disclosure or nakedness that marriage requires. The kind of trust God saw in Adam and Eve was superior to all else because they had achieved such a level of oneness that being naked around each other felt no different than if each were in his or her own private bathroom and naked. Adam and Eve had no inhibition, shame or discomfort. The trust observed in the text is the ultimate expression of intimacy; it conveys the message that I feel safe in showing and sharing my strengths as well as my imperfections with this one person. It's being confident that my vulnerabilities will be protected.

I firmly believe that it is God's intent that this level of intimacy be reserved for just that one special person, my friend, my lover, my wife/husband. Being together and naked says I've got your back and you've got mine. Like all the other legs, this level of trust is achieved over time. It must evolve naturally in an environment of consistency and in the company of one. That one person must be faithful, always making you their number one priority. That person must be honest and must always tell the truth in a loving and caring manner. He/she must love unconditionally and should be ready to make the necessary sacrifice. That person must be respectful and be accountable to their spouse. That person must be forgiving and willing to leave the past in the past. That person must be one of moral integrity, practice what they preach, and do the right thing. If each person in the marriage chooses to be that one person, then trust will thrive in the marriage. Trust is so delicate that it must be closely guarded because though it can take years to build, it can be destroyed in an instant. As with the other three legs of the loveseat, the level of trust determines the level of comfort and fulfillment that the loveseat or marriage will provide.

Every marriage has its level of trust and there are certain indicators that reveal where that level is. One such indicator is the use of prenuptial agreements. Some years ago, prenuptial agreements were almost exclusively used by the rich and famous. Today, they are becoming more and more popular among the middle class. While I understand the concept and utility of prenuptial agreements, they really are legal safeguards erected when trust is questionable. A prenuptial is one spouse saying to the next "I trust you with my body, but I don't trust you with my heart." You may be asking why I say heart instead of money. Well, Jesus said in St. Matthew 6:21, "For where your treasure is, there your heart [your wishes, your desires; that on which your life centers] will be also." (AMP). A prenuptial agreement is a polite way of saying I do not trust that you will always do what is in my best interest; I suspect that given the chance you will run off with my money and my stuff. To put it quite bluntly, if you can trust somebody with your money, you can probably trust him or her with your life. Considering how short life is, why would anyone want to spend their lifetime tied to somebody they do not trust with their life? Sadly, many of us do.

Some couples do not sign official prenuptial agreements but still practice the same measure of distrust by the way they compartmentalize their resources. When couples insist on labeling everything into groups of "his" and "hers," then those are likely indicators that trust is an issue in the marriage. When trust is active in the marriage, there is rarely the need to label things. In my own home, for example, none of the vehicles are exclusively mine or my wife's. In fact, we always joke that the newer vehicle is always my wife's, as I am always more concerned about her safety and comfort than my own. Whichever vehicle we both drive on any given day is really more of a practical matter than an indication of ownership. We have always owned everything together because trust makes that practice the only way to go.

Money Answers All Things

Matthew 6:21 reveals that trust and treasure are inextricably linked and your loveseat will not be all it is designed to be without them. The final portion of this book, therefore, will focus on the area that sometimes breeds the most anxiety and mistrust in a marriage. It is the area of treasure, more popularly known as money. Why is money so important? Money is a key that unlocks many doors and empowers us to do things and go places. Money can determine people's quality of life during their working years, and, more importantly, when they retire. It is money that has given you ownership of this book that you are reading. Solomon, in Ecclesiastes 10:19 says, "Money answereth all things." (KJV). With so much riding on money, one can well imagine why it is so important in marriages. Trust in this area is critical to the proper functioning of the loveseat. Trust with money is twofold. Firstly, it has to do with trusting the management skills of the assigned money manager in the marriage. Secondly, it has to do with trusting that the manager will never run off with the money or be selfish with it; it involves trust that the manager will never forget that the two have become one.

Money through the Ages

You may have heard the following statement being batted about from time to time: "His money is her money and her money is her money." This statement jokingly implies that all the money belongs to the wife. But if the two have become one flesh, then all the money, irrespective of who brings it in, belongs to the couple. Let's take a walk down the corridors of history to see how money has been handled down through the ages. Atwood in *"Couples and Money: The Last Taboo,"* referenced research that tracked the historic influence and meaning of money in a marriage in America. It showed that men's greatest power in the marriage in the 1800's came from their status as breadwinners. Men were responsible for the financial support of the entire family. Women were raised to be financially dependent, taking care of the home and raising the children. As a result, the men were the uncontested head in the marriage as they were viewed as having the sole right to control the money. This hierarchy began to erode as wives began contributing to the financial lives of their homes. By the mid twentieth century, America had experienced two world wars and the Great Depression, which led to the entry of a large number of women into the workforce. This trend only continued after the wars were over and by the 1990's, according to Atwood, wives' contribution to the household increased to 40% (Atwood). Today, it is not strange to find households where the wife brings in most of the income. It is important that people, especially men, understand that times have changed and customs have evolved. As more and more women enter the workforce, the notion that the husband is the automatic money manager in the household has fallen by the wayside. In many marriages, that decision is now based on who is the more competent money manager.

Men, Money and the Emotional Connection

Men who see themselves as providers have stronger feelings about their earnings than do women. Their identities and feelings of worth are often tied to their earnings; and therefore they associate success with their ability to provide. At their core, men have, and will always be hunters; their earnings represent the kill, and the kill validates their manhood. Understanding the above is quite critical in helping men adjust to reduced income or total loss of a job, as many are likely to interpret this as an attack on their manhood and may experience the erosion of their self worth as a result. One other occurrence that can yield a similar result is when the wife begins to earn more than the husband. On its own merit, increased income is a good thing, but some men have difficulty handling it because they think their position of power is threatened, even if the wife has no intention of disrupting the order. It is here that a husband must trust that his wife has his back and that she takes pleasure in making him look good.

Another problem that can arise when the wife joins her husband in the work force is that some husbands do not make any adjustments in helping in the home and with the children. So, while she steps in to help him bring in the funds, he refuses to step up and help her on the home front. If this is not addressed quickly, his wife will soon become resentful and may view him as unloving and insensitive.

After a while, the wife may begin to question whether the husband is even necessary, since she is doing all the work at home and bringing in money as well.

Letting Go So I Can Grow

People's relationship with money during childhood often impacts their approach to it in marriage. In his book "Rich Dad Poor Dad" the multi millionaire Robert Kiyosaki speaks about how many self made millionaires use their poverty-stricken upbringing as a motivation to get wealth. He also cautions against allowing the fear of poverty to dominate one's life, because the pursuit of wealth can become an addiction whereby no amount of money will ever be enough. In that case, money will become a slave master and not a tool to enjoy life. Others who emerge from humble beginnings sometimes use money to mask personal insecurity and self esteem issues. Take Kirkland, for example. Kirkland grew up in the inner city, and was constantly teased by his peers at school because his parents could never afford to get him a good pair of shoes. He survived the horrors of high school but experienced constant rejection from would be employers once they found out where he lived. Luckily for Kirkland, he obtained a visa, came to America, and worked his way up the ladder at his job. Kirkland pledged to himself that nobody would ever laugh at his shoes or clothes ever again. He developed a habit of spending most of his earnings on new shoes and clothes because they made him feel important. Now, Kirkland is married to Christine, and she is concerned about her husband's constant buying of shoes and clothes that he does not need. She fears he is a shopaholic and worries that he is shopping away their future. He, on the other hand, resents her because he feels that she is trying to deprive him of something he's worked hard to buy with his own money. Kirkland is attempting to use money and material goods to fix a shattered self-image but is only succeeding in tearing his marriage apart. His poor relationship with money causes him to spend it in order to appear rich, but his actions will result in his family being very poor. Sadly, there are a lot of married Kirklands (male and female) in the world today, who spend unwisely on things they cannot afford, such as: jewelry, cars, boats, houses etc. To break the cycle, Kirkland has to be willing to be naked before his wife by facing his insecurities rather than continuing to mask them with stuff. He must trust that the only people that really matter are the two in the marriage. It is the letting go of the past that will allow him to grow.

Growing up poor can have the opposite effect as well. It can cause people to become hoarders who are unwilling to spend on things that are necessary. As with sex, money has the potential to become a tool of punishment or reward. When this happens, the affected spouse may feel personally rejected, unloved, unwanted, or taken for granted, as spending becomes synonymous with affection and love. The key here is a balanced and responsible approach to spending. Sometimes couples make the mistake of not being responsible with their spending simply because they feel they do not make enough money to warrant taking special care of it. This, however, only lays the foundation for future frustration because if the income increases but the spending habits remain the same, the couple will most likely find themselves in greater debt.

The way people handle money is correlated to their degree of indebtedness and creditworthiness. Considering how important a role credit plays in America today, if a husband and wife are not on the same page, one may feel that his or her effort to get out of debt is rendered futile by the other's impulsive and often unnecessary spending habits. It is gravely important that all major spending decisions be made together. I am reminded of a couple who had just purchased a new home. The husband has always been a strong believer in buying furniture with cash, even if it takes a while. The wife, on the other hand, was more concerned about the impression their friends would have if they visited and saw the house sparse. She decided to go out and purchase a new bedroom set on credit, without her husband's knowledge. The deliverymen showed up and something rather embarrassing happened; the furniture that the wife picked out was too big for their bedroom. Everything had to be returned to the store; a restocking fee was charged and a husband's trust was violated. If she had included her husband (who is a building contractor) in the process, he would have considered dimensions as a criterion in choosing the furniture and they would have avoided the embarrassment of choosing items that did not fit.

Different Strokes for Different Folks

Every couple must decide on a money management style that works
for them. Below, I have included the four that Atwood believes are
most common:

1) **Whole wage**—one gives all or most of their income to
the other who uses it, plus any income of their own, to
cover the household expenses.

2) **Housekeeping allowance**—the breadwinner gives the
partner money to cover the household finances and
retains control of the rest.

3) **Pooling system**—all or almost all of the household
income is combined, usually in a joint account, and both
partners, at least in principle, contribute to the financial
management.

4) **Independent management**—both partners have a
separate source of income and either split the household
finances or each pay for certain household expenses.

A fifth approach that is becoming more and more popular expands on the Pooling system. Instead of having one account, the couple establishes four: one for savings, one for all bills, one for the husband and the other for the wife. Once the bills are cleared, a set amount goes into savings and the rest is divided equally and allocated to the "his" and "hers" accounts. Both spouses are given full authority over their respective accounts to do whatever they want without impacting the general functioning of the household. It also gives the couple the sense that they are not just working to pay bills but are personally rewarded for their hard work. The approach that any couple chooses is going to be dependent on the dynamics at play in the home. However, I tend to like option four (4) the least as it gives the impression that the wife and husband are two separate entities who just happen to share the same address. It engenders an environment of independence rather than interdependence, which is not conducive to trust but rather gives rise to suspicion.

Additionally, it is wise to have the better money manager handle the money but that person must always keep the other aware, so that if he/she becomes incapacitated or dies, the other spouse knows enough to pick up and continue without everything falling apart. Being a pastor, I have come across a few situations where the money manager dies and the spouse is left with grief and bewilderment because throughout the marriage, they were totally unaware of their liabilities and their assets. There were some cases where the remaining spouse never even knew what bills needed to be paid and when. I must point out here that while the trust factor is admirable, this does not preclude the person not managing the money from being informed because, in this case, what you don't know can certainly hurt you.

Everybody Needs a Coach

One of my favorite things to say to couples that I counsel with is this: If Lebron James, one of the greatest basket ball player of all times, needs several coaches, then every couple should have coaches to help them in areas of their marriage. Many couples struggle in the area of money management due to misinformation or experiences they had while growing up. Those who do should get a good coach/financial adviser to help them cut through all the emotional "red tape" and allow them to really focus on the strategies and practices that will give them a solid financial footing. Couples can also educate themselves by investing in books and attending seminars that specifically deal with the issue of money. God expects the couple to be naked and unashamed around each other; He expects to see trust, the final leg of the loveseat in place. Trust around the issue of money becomes easier when there is a clear strategy, good communication and a keen sense of oneness. If the couple struggles in any of the above areas, then they should seek help early so as to prevent bad habits from forming and to avoid frustration and conflict within the marriage.

NOTES

6

LAST WORDS

I t is quite clear that there are some critical pieces needed to make a marriage healthy. Although we may not have perfect mastery over all four mentioned in this book, a good place to begin is to be fully aware of the potential impact that each can have on a marriage. While some believe marriages are made in heaven, we have to work them out here on earth. They require investment; each couple chooses either to invest in their loveseat incrementally or pay dearly at the end for a marriage that failed. Always remember that your marriage is what you make it. While there are some merits in admiring great marriages, never make yours a duplicate, but insist on creating your own. When you run into unexpected turbulence, which you will sometimes do, go back to the Manual and consult with the

Inventor. There you will find answers to improve this glorious love seat called marriage. My friends, I do wish for you everything good in your marriage. Take good care of it, and it may last you for the rest of your life.

A PRAYER AND BLESSING FOR YOUR MARRIAGE

Throughout this book, I have placed emphasis on consulting the Instructional Manual that the Creator has given us to navigate challenges that arise in marriage. At this point, I also wish to strongly encourage you to habitually consult with the Creator of marriage about your marriage. Pray always for your marriage, in good and bad times. Below you will find a prayer, which is by no means a formula, but will help you get started. When you pray, always do so with confidence, knowing that the Creator wants your marriage to succeed. Please take a moment to pray the following:

Dear Lord Jesus, I come to you now on behalf of my spouse and I. Lord, I pray today that our marriage will be strong and impenetrable. I plead the Blood of Jesus against every opposition that seeks to diminish or weaken this holy union of husband and wife. I declare today that no weapon formed against us shall prosper, and I condemn every tongue that rises up against us. May the darts of the enemy miss their target; may every plot against us come to sudden defeat. Lord Jesus, cause our marriage to grow stronger through each trial; may the bond between us, as husband and wife, grow deeper with every storm. May we emerge as an example and an encouragement to many others, as we demonstrate Jesus' love for His Church by our love and commitment to each other. Lord, may we become better individuals because of each other's love and support. Father, may we rise together each day fully persuaded that we are highly favored by you because you have blessed us with each other. Make our home a place of solace, refreshment, relaxation and pleasure. May we enjoy each other's company like no other, and may our bond of love never be tampered with or broken. Lord, cause our children, family and friends to call us blessed in Jesus' name. Amen.

My friends, today, I decree a blessing over your marriage. May God bless the fruit of your womb/loins and the fruit of your hands. May God block every attack of barrenness, sickness and poverty; may He guide you through every valley and sustain you during every dry season. I command your marriage to survive, to thrive, and to succeed; I declare your marriage blessed in Jesus' name! Amen.

REFERENCES

Atwood, J.D. "Couples and Money: The Last Taboo." *The American Journal of Family Therapy*. 40 (2012): 1-19.

Chapman, Gary. *The Five Love Languages: The Secret to Love that Lasts*. Chicago: Northfield, 1992. Print.

English Standard Version (ESV). Bible Gateway. Web. 17 Dec. 2015.

Kiyosaki, Robert. *Rich Dad, Poor Dad: What the Rich Teach Their Kids about Money That the Poor and Middle Class Do Not*. New York: Warner, (1997). Print.

Hunt, J. *Biblical Counseling Keys: Communication, The Heart of the Matter*. Database © 2009 WORD*search* Corp.

Litzinger, S., Gordon, K.C. "Exploring Relationship Among Communication, Sexual Satisfaction, and Marital Satisfaction." *Journal of Sex & Marital Therapy*. 31 (2005): 409-424.

The Amplified Bible (AMP). Bible Gateway. Web. 17 Dec. 2015.

The King James Bible (KJV). Bible Gateway. Web. 17 Dec. 2015.

The Message Bible (MSG). Bible Gateway. Web. 17 Dec. 2015.

Andrew C. Daubon

ABOUT THE AUTHOR

Andrew C. Daubon has been happily married to Michaelia Daubon, whom he affectionately refers to as the eighth wonder of the world, for over 15 years and are proud parents of two daughters.

Andrew serves with his wife as pastors of the Celestial Praise Church of God in Springfield MA. He is an Ordained Bishop with the Church of God; District Overseer for the Springfield District of Churches, Secretary of the Pastor's Council of Greater Springfield and serves as a member of the Southern New England Regional State Council.

Andrew is a graduate of the Mico College University, in Kingston, Jamaica and the University of Hartford, in West Hartford, CT. He is currently pursuing a Master of Divinity at the Gordon Conwell Theological Seminary. He has been providing Bible based premarital and marital counseling to his congregation, local community, nationwide and Jamaica for a number of years. He and his wife conduct marriage workshops for churches by invitation. He believes that marriage was made by God to be enjoyed, not endured.

Andrew takes a practical approach to trouble shooting the challenges that arise in marriage and firmly believes that the quality of every marriage is a direct result of the effort invested into it by both spouses.

For bookings, questions or comments he can be reached at
DaubonOffice@CuriouslyFormed.com
CuriouslyFormed@gmail.com
www.curiouslyformed.com